Duckology Trivia Challenge

Oregon Ducks Football

Duckology Trivia Challenge – Oregon Ducks Football;
First Edition 2008

Published by
Kick The Ball, Ltd
8595 Columbus Pike, Suite 197
Lewis Center, OH 43035
www.TriviaGameBooks.com

Designed, Formatted, and Edited by: Tom P. Rippey III & Paul F. Wilson
Researched by: Billy Wilcox

For information on ordering this book in bulk at reduced prices, please email us at pfwilson@trivianthology.com.

International Standard Book Number: 978-1-934372-47-0

Printed & Bound in the United States of America

Tom P. Rippey III & Paul F. Wilson

Duckology Trivia Challenge

Oregon Ducks Football

Researched by Billy Wilcox

Tom P. Rippey III & Paul F. Wilson, Editors

Kick The Ball, Ltd
Lewis Center, Ohio

This book is dedicated to our families and friends for your unwavering love, support, and your understanding of our pursuit of our passions. Thank you for everything you do for us and for making our lives complete.

Dear Friend,

Thank you for purchasing our ***Duckology Trivia Challenge*** game book!

We hope you enjoy it as much as we enjoyed researching and putting it together. This book can be used over and over again in many different ways. One example would be to use it in a head-to-head challenge by alternating questions between Duck football fans – or by playing as teams. Another option would be to simply challenge yourself to see how many questions you could answer correctly. No matter how you choose to use this book, you'll have fun and maybe even learn a fact or two about Ducks football.

We have made every attempt to verify the accuracy of the questions and answers contained in this book. However it is still possible that from time to time an error has been made by us or our researchers. In the event you find a question or answer that is questionable or inaccurate, we ask for your understanding and thank you for bringing it to our attention so that we may improve future editions of this book. Please email us at tprippey@trivianthology.com with those observations and comments.

Have fun playing ***Duckology Trivia Challenge***!

Tom & Paul

Tom Rippey & Paul Wilson
Co-Founders, Kick The Ball, Ltd

PS – You can discover more about all of our current trivia game books by visiting us online at www.TriviaGameBooks.com.

Table of Contents

DUCKOLOGY TRIVIA CHALLENGE

How to Play

Book Format:

There are four quarters, each made up of fifty questions. Each quarter's questions have assigned point values. Questions are designed to get progressively more difficult as you proceed through each quarter, as well as through the book itself. Most questions are in a four-option multiple-choice format so you will at least have a 25% chance of getting a correct answer for some of the more challenging questions.

We've even added an *Overtime* section in the event of a tie, or just in case you want to keep playing a little longer.

Game Options:

One Player -
To play on your own, simply answer each of the questions in all the quarters, and in the overtime section, if you'd like. Use the *Player / Team Score Sheet* to record your answers and the quarter *Answer Keys* to check your answers. Calculate each quarter's points and the total for the game at the bottom of the *Player / Team Score Sheet* to determine your final score.

Two or More Players –
To play with multiple players decide if you will all be competing with each other individually, or if you will form and play as teams. Each player / team will then have its own *Player / Team Score Sheet* to record its answer. You can use the quarter *Answer Keys* to check your answers and to calculate your final scores.

The *Player / Team Score Sheets* have been designed so that each team can answer all questions or you can divide the questions up in any combination you would prefer. For example, you may want to alternate questions if two players are playing or answer every third question for three players, etc. In any case, simply record your response to your questions in the corresponding quarter and question number on the *Player / Team Score Sheet*.

A winner will be determined by multiplying the total number of correct answers for each quarter by the point value per quarter, then adding together the final total for all quarters combined. Play the game again and again by alternating the questions that your team is assigned so that you will answer a different set of questions each time you play.

You Create the Game -
There are countless other ways of using ***Duckology Trivia Challenge*** questions. It's limited only to your imagination. Examples might be using them at your tailgate or other college football related party. Players / Teams who answer questions incorrectly may have to perform a required action, or winners may receive special prizes. Let us know what other games you come up with!

Have fun!

First Quarter

1-Point Questions

1) In which city is the University of Oregon located?

A) Portland
B) Medford
C) Salem
D) Eugene

2) What are the Ducks' official colors?

A) Green and Yellow
B) Scarlet and White
C) Black and Gold
D) Red, White and Blue

3) Oregon's stadium has a seating capacity of over 60,000.

A) True
B) False

4) What year did Oregon play its first game?

A) 1894
B) 1905
C) 1912
D) 1926

5) How many members make up the Oregon Marching Band?

A) 160
B) 190
C) 210
D) 240

6) What is the name of the award given each season to Oregon's most outstanding player?

A) Duck Feather
B) Hoffman Award
C) Oregon Star
D) Gold Plaque

7) How many games did Oregon win in 2007?

A) 6
B) 7
C) 8
D) 9

8) Which Ducks head coach had the longest tenure?

A) Mike Bellotti
B) Len Casanova
C) Rich Brooks
D) Jerry Frei

9) Who was the first player from Oregon to be picked number one in the NFL Draft?

A) Akili Smith
B) George Shaw
C) Bobby Moore
D) Joey Harrington

10) By what other name is the Oregon-Oregon State game known?

A) Oregon Showdown
B) Northwest Cup
C) Battle of the Pacific
D) Civil War

11) How many Heisman Trophies have been won by Oregon players?

A) 0
B) 1
C) 3
D) 4

12) Does Oregon have a winning record against Washington?

A) Yes
B) No

13) What is the name of Oregon's mascot?

A) Buster
B) Donald
C) Tommy
D) Rocky

14) How many overtime games did Oregon play in 2007?

A) 1
B) 2
C) 3
D) 4

15) In which season did Oregon first receive an *AP* Top-25 ranking?

A) 1940
B) 1948
C) 1955
D) 1962

16) Who was Oregon's first head coach?

A) Frank Simpson
B) Bill Warner
C) Cal Young
D) Tex Oliver

17) Who holds the Oregon record for career receptions?

A) Bobby Moore
B) Sammie Parker
C) Keenen Howry
D) Bob Newland

18) Which team handed Oregon its worst (most points) all-time defeat?

A) Washington
B) Oklahoma
C) Texas
D) UCLA

19) Who holds the career rushing record at Oregon?

A) Onterrio Smith
B) Reuben Droughns
C) Saladin McCollough
D) Derek Loville

20) Who was the Ducks' first All-American?

A) Jake Leicht
B) Mel Renfro
C) Shy Huntington
D) Norm Van Brocklin

21) What is the name of the University of Oregon's fight song?

A) Rock On
B) Go, Fight, Win
C) Disco Duck
D) Mighty Oregon

22) Who led Oregon in receiving yards in 2007?

A) Jaison Williams
B) Cameron Colvin
C) Ed Dickson
D) Garren Strong

23) Which Oregon head coach has the most wins as a Duck?

A) Len Casanova
B) Mike Bellotti
C) Don Read
D) Rich Brooks

24) What year did Oregon join the Pac-10 Conference?

A) 1948
B) 1952
C) 1964
D) 1971

25) Who holds the record for passing yards in a single game at Oregon?

A) Bill Musgrave
B) Dan Fouts
C) Norm Van Brocklin
D) Joey Harrington

26) What is awarded to the winner of the Oregon-Oregon State game?

A) Victory Bell
B) Silver Horseshoe
C) Platypus Trophy
D) Wooden Bucket

27) Which U.S. Service Academy is the only one that has defeated Oregon?

A) Air Force
B) Army
C) Navy
D) Never lost to a U.S. Service Academy

28) Which defender led Oregon in pass interceptions in 2007?

A) Matthew Harper
B) Patrick Chung
C) Walter Thurmond
D) Jairus Byrd

29) Does Oregon have a winning record in homecoming games?

A) Yes
B) No

30) Who holds the Oregon record for all-purpose yards in a single game?

A) Pat Johnson
B) Don Reynolds
C) Onterrio Smith
D) Bobby Moore

31) Who led the Ducks in sacks in 2007?

A) Nick Reed
B) Will Tukuafu
C) Jeremy Gibbs
D) Kenny Rowe

32) Who was Oregon's opponent in their first game at Autzen Stadium?

A) Ohio State
B) Nebraska
C) Arkansas
D) Colorado

33) Why did Oregon not field a football team for the 1943 and 1944 seasons?

A) No football budget
B) Lack of fan support
C) World War II
D) Poor academic performance

34) How many winning seasons has Oregon had?

A) 46
B) 57
C) 64
D) 70

35) How many Oregon players were named 1st team All Pac-10 in 2007?

A) 2
B) 3
C) 5
D) 7

36) Who was the first two-time All-American for Oregon?

A) Mel Renfro
B) John Kitzmiller
C) Jim Shanley
D) Steve Barnett

37) Who was the last Duck to lead the team in tackles for three straight seasons?

A) Peter Simon
B) Joe Farwell
C) Bruce Beekley
D) Chad Cota

38) Who holds the Oregon record for consecutive field goals made?

A) Kirk Dennis
B) Stan Woodfill
C) Jared Siegel
D) Tommy Thompson

39) Who was Oregon's opponent in their first ever overtime game?

A) Fresno State
B) California
C) Stanford
D) Utah

40) Does Oregon have a winning record against USC?

A) Yes
B) No

41) What is the highest *AP* ranking Oregon has received in the final poll?

A) #2
B) #4
C) #5
D) #7

42) Who holds the Oregon record for receiving yards in a season?

A) Bobby Moore
B) Keenan Howry
C) Demetrius Williams
D) Bob Newland

43) How many touchdown passes did Dennis Dixon throw in 2007?

A) 14
B) 17
C) 20
D) 22

44) How many Pac-10 Championships has Oregon won?

A) 3
B) 5
C) 7
D) 9

45) Which player holds the single game rushing record at Oregon?

A) Tony Cherry
B) Ricky Whittle
C) Jonathan Stewart
D) Onterrio Smith

46) Who was the first All-American wide receiver at Oregon?

A) Bob Newland
B) Lew Barnes
C) Terry Obee
D) Sammie Parker

47) How many Oregon head coaches lasted just one season?

A) 4
B) 7
C) 10
D) 13

48) What award did Oregon's Haloti Ngata win in 2005?

A) Outland Trophy
B) Nagurski Award
C) Morris Trophy
D) Lombardi Award

49) Who holds the Oregon career record for points scored?

A) Bobby Moore
B) Jared Siegel
C) Terrence Whitehead
D) Joshua Smith

50) In which year did the Ducks first celebrate a victory over Oregon State?

A) 1895
B) 1901
C) 1906
D) 1910

First Quarter Duck Cool Fact

During the 1840s, the ancestors of a group of Massachusetts fishermen known as The Webfoots settled in the Williamette Valley. This prompted the State of Oregon to adopt the motto "The Webfoot State". Oregon students took a liking to the name and began referring to themselves as Webfoots. Oregon sportswriters, seeking an alternative term, began using Ducks. Oregon held a student vote and chose Ducks as their new nickname over Timberwolves and Lumberjacks. In 1932, a second student vote was held and the Ducks nickname prevailed once again, beating out Trappers, Pioneers and Yellowjackets. Oregon remains the only major University to carry the Ducks nickname, and until the Anaheim NHL franchise appeared in 1993, there were no professional sports teams to be called Ducks.

First Quarter Answer Key

1) D – Eugene (The University of Oregon, founded in 1867, is located in Eugene, Oregon. Eugene is named after its founder Eugene Franklin Skinner and is the 3rd most populated city in the state.)
2) A – Green and Yellow (The official colors of the Ducks are green and yellow. Oregon, however, has become known for their many uniform combinations, which have included black, grey, and white along with the official green and yellow.)
3) B – False (Oregon's Autzen Stadium has an official capacity of 54,000, though actual attendance frequently exceeds that number.)
4) A – 1894 (Oregon's first game was played in 1894, a 44-2 victory over Albany College.)
5) D – 240 (The Oregon Marching Band [OMB] has 240 members, making it the largest student group on campus.)
6) B – Hoffman Award (The Hoffman Award is presented each year to the team's most outstanding player based on a team vote. Bob Smith was the recipient of the first Hoffman Award in 1939.)
7) D – 9 (The Ducks finished the 2007 season with a 9-4 record.)

8) C – Rich Brooks (Brooks spent 18 seasons at Oregon from 1977-1994.)
9) B – George Shaw (Oregon QB George Shaw was selected #1 overall in 1955 by the Baltimore Colts.)
10) D – Civil War (The "Civil War" nickname was first used in reference to the game in 1929 and came into common use in 1937.)
11) A – 0 (Joey Harrington became the first Heisman Trophy finalist in Oregon history in 2001, finishing 4th.)
12) B – No (Oregon is 37-58-5 all-time versus Washington.)
13) B – Donald (Oregon was granted permission to use the likeness of Disney's Donald Duck in the 1940s when athletic director Leo Harris reached an informal handshake agreement with Walt Disney. It was put into writing in 1973.)
14) A – 1 (Oregon beat Oregon State 38-31 in 2 OTs.)
15) B – 1984 (Oregon cracked the Top-25 for the first time in October of 1948, coming in at #14.)
16) C – Cal Young (Young led Oregon to a 1-2-1 record in 1894.)
17) B – Sammie Parker (Parker caught 178 passes in his Oregon career, which spanned from 2000-2003.)
18) A – Washington (The Huskies beat Oregon 66-0 in 1974.)

19) D – Derek Loville (Loville had 811 carries for 3,444 yards at Oregon from 1986-1989.)

20) C – Shy Huntington (1916)

21) D – Mighty Oregon (Director of Bands Albert Perfect co-wrote the song with student Dewitt Gilbert. It was first performed in 1916.)

22) A – Jaison Williams (Williams had 55 catches for 844 yards and 8 touchdowns in 2007.)

23) B – Mike Bellotti (Bellotti's 106 wins ranks #1 all-time at Oregon.)

24) C – 1964 (Oregon joined the Pac-10 [then called the Athletic Association of Western Universities] in 1964, along with Oregon State.)

25) A – Bill Musgrave (Musgrave threw for 489 yards at BYU in 1989. Oregon 41, BYU 45)

26) C – Platypus Trophy (The trophy was created by art student Warren Spady and was awarded from 1959-1961. The trophy was "lost" for more than 40 years and found in 2005. It was awarded again in 2007.)

27) A – Air Force (Oregon is 8-3-1 all-time versus Air Force.)

28) D – Jairus Byrd (Byrd recorded 7 interceptions during the 2007 season.)

29) A – Yes (Oregon is 30-29-3 all-time on homecoming, including a 53-7 victory over Washington State in 2007.)

30) C – Onterrio Smith (Smith totaled 342 yards [285 Rushing, 57 return yards] at Washington State in 2001.)

31) A – Nick Reed (Reed recorded 12 sacks for a loss of 101 yards in 2007.)

32) D – Colorado (Oregon lost to Colorado 13-17 in September of 1967.)

33) C – World War II (Oregon did not field a team in 1943 and 1944 due to World War II.)

34) B – 57 (Oregon has had 57 winning seasons since 1894.)

35) C – 5 (QB Dennis Dixon, RB Jonathan Stewart, OL Max Unger, DL Nick Reed, and DB Patrick Chung)

36) D – Steve Barnett (The Oregon tackle earned All-America honors in 1961 and 1962.)

37) B – Joe Farwell (Farwell led the Ducks with 112 tackles in 1990, 100 tackles in 1991, and 110 tackles in 1992.)

38) C – Jared Siegel (Siegel connected on 15 straight field goal attempts in 2002.)

39) A – Fresno State (Oregon beat Fresno State 30-27 in 1996.)

40) B – No (Oregon is 16-36-2 all-time versus USC.)

41) A – #2 (Oregon finished the 2001 season ranked #2, the highest ranking ever in the history of Oregon football.)
42) D – Bob Newland (Newland caught 67 passes for 1,123 yards and 7 touchdowns in 1970.)
43) C – 20 (Dixon threw 20 touchdown passes in 2007, despite missing the last 3 games with a left knee injury.)
44) A – 3 (1994, 2000, and 2001)
45) D – Onterrio Smith (Smith rushed for 285 yards on 26 carries at Washington State in 2001.)
46) A – Bob Newland (1970)
47) D – 13 (Oregon has had 13 coaches last just one season: Cal Young [1894], Percy Benson [1895], J.F. Frick [1896], Joe Smith [1897], Lawrence Kaarsberg [1900], Marion Dolph [1902], R.S. Smith [1904], Bruce Shorts [1905], Gordon Frost [1907], Louis Pinkham [1912], Joe Maddock [1924], Richard Smith [1925], and John Warren [1942].)
48) C – Morris Trophy (Ngata won the award as the Pac-10's top defensive lineman after recording 61 tackles [9 for loss] and 3 sacks in 2005.)

49) B – Jared Siegel (Siegel scored 323 points at Oregon from 2001-2004.)

50) A – 1895 (Oregon 44, Oregon State 0)

Note: All answers valid as of the end of the 2007 season, unless otherwise indicated in the question itself.

Second Quarter *2-Point Questions*

1) What are the most points ever scored in a season by an Oregon team?

A) 410
B) 456
C) 496
D) 528

2) What number did Ricky Whittle wear at Oregon?

A) 14
B) 22
C) 28
D) 33

3) How many Oregon players are in the College Football Hall of Fame?

A) 1
B) 2
C) 4
D) 6

4) How many times has Oregon scored 50+ points in a game?

A) 16
B) 27
C) 38
D) 49

Second Quarter *2-Point Questions*

5) Terrence Whitehead led the Ducks in rushing for three straight seasons?

A) True
B) False

6) How many times has Oregon finished the season undefeated?

A) 2
B) 3
C) 4
D) 5

7) When was the first time the Ducks traveled out-of-state for a game?

A) 1895
B) 1899
C) 1904
D) 1910

8) Which U.S. Service Academy has Oregon never played?

A) Air Force
B) Army
C) Navy
D) Played all three

9) Has an Oregon team ever rushed for 500 yards in a game?

A) Yes
B) No

10) Which school has Oregon played less than 20 times?

A) San Jose State
B) Utah
C) Idaho
D) Arizona State

11) What is Oregon's winning percentage against Oregon State?

A) .495
B) .541
C) .577
D) .623

12) Who holds the Oregon record for most passing yards in a bowl game?

A) Kellen Clemens
B) Chris Miller
C) Akili Smith
D) Danny O'Neil

13) How many times has Oregon hosted ESPN's *College Gameday*?

A) 3
B) 5
C) 7
D) 9

14) What year was the first 10-win season at Oregon?

A) 1962
B) 1988
C) 2000
D) 2007

15) What is the record for most points scored by Oregon against Oregon State?

A) 35
B) 42
C) 49
D) 56

16) Who holds the Oregon record for career pass interceptions?

A) Chris Oldham
B) George Shaw
C) Mario Clark
D) Jake Leicht

17) How many yards is the longest pass play in Oregon history?

A) 68
B) 80
C) 95
D) 99

18) What award is given each year to Oregon's top defensive lineman?

A) Joe Scheffeld Award
B) Duck Defender Trophy
C) Elite Duck Defender
D) Ed Moshofsky Award

19) How many Oregon players have been selected in the first round of the NFL Draft?

A) 5
B) 6
C) 8
D) 12

20) The Ducks have won more than 10 bowl games.

A) True
B) False

Second Quarter *2-Point Questions*

21) Who was the first Oregon quarterback to throw for 2,000 yards in a season?

A) Tony Graziani
B) Tom Blanchard
C) Dan Fouts
D) Chris Miller

22) In which bowl was Oregon's first bowl appearance?

A) Cotton Bowl
B) Blue Bonnet Bowl
C) Liberty Bowl
D) Rose Bowl

23) When was the first time Oregon had two players with 100 yards receiving in the same game?

A) 1950
B) 1965
C) 1979
D) 1992

24) Who holds the Oregon record for field goals made in a season?

A) Gregg McCallum
B) Nathan Villegas
C) Tommy Thompson
D) Jared Siegel

25) In which season did Oregon average the most rushing yards per game?

A) 1955
B) 1971
C) 1989
D) 2004

26) What year did Oregon win its first conference championship?

A) 1919
B) 1927
C) 1943
D) 1961

27) How many times has Oregon finished the season ranked in the Top-10 of the *AP* Poll?

A) 2
B) 3
C) 4
D) 6

28) Oregon All-American RB Mel Renfro was also named All-American in what other sport?

A) Wrestling
B) Basketball
C) Track and Field
D) Baseball

29) Where did Oregon Coach Mike Bellotti play college football?

A) Montana
B) Arkansas
C) UC Davis
D) Weber State

30) How many games did Oregon play in its first season?

A) 4
B) 6
C) 8
D) 10

31) Who owns the Oregon record for most receiving yards in a single game against Oregon State?

A) Bob Newland
B) Tony Hartley
C) Damon Griffin
D) Pat Johnson

32) Against which BCS Conference does Oregon have the best winning percentage?

A) Big 12
B) SEC
C) Big East
D) Big Ten

33) Who has the most rushing yards for Oregon in a single game against USC?

A) Jack Morris
B) Saladin McCollough
C) Don Reynolds
D) Derek Loville

34) Who was the first Oregon QB to pass for 1,000 yards in back-to-back seasons?

A) Bill Musgrave
B) Bob Berry
C) George Shaw
D) Dan Fouts

35) To which team did Oregon suffer its first ever loss?

A) Portland
B) California
C) Albany
D) Oregon State

36) In which year did Oregon have two players selected in the first round of the NFL Draft?

A) 1963
B) 1972
C) 1991
D) 2002

37) When was the last season an Oregon defense gave up less than 10 points per game?

A) 1964
B) 1972
C) 1983
D) 1991

38) How many times did Sean Burwell rush for 100 yards in his Oregon career?

A) 6
B) 8
C) 11
D) 14

39) Who holds the Oregon record for passing yards in a season?

A) Chris Miller
B) Akili Smith
C) Bill Musgrave
D) Joey Harrington

40) Oregon's Bobby Moore led the Pac-10 in receiving and scoring in 1969.

A) True
B) False

41) Who holds the Oregon single game receiving yards record?

A) Blake Spence
B) Demetrius Williams
C) Tony Hartley
D) Derrick Deadwiler

42) How many Duck players have had over 1,000 yards receiving in a single season?

A) 2
B) 4
C) 5
D) 7

43) Who was the first All-American defensive back at Oregon?

A) Jake Leicht
B) Chad Cota
C) Jim Smith
D) Alex Molden

44) How many outright Pac-10 Championships has Oregon won?

A) 0
B) 2
C) 4
D) 6

45) How many Oregon players have had their jersey number retired?

A) 0
B) 1
C) 2
D) 4

46) How many points did Oregon score in its first season?

A) 32
B) 44
C) 58
D) 69

47) Who is the only Oregon player to kick 6 field goals in a game?

A) Jared Siegel
B) Matt Belden
C) Paul Martinez
D) Josh Frankel

48) Which of these Oregon coaches is the only one to win his first game at Oregon?

A) Len Casanova
B) Don Read
C) Rich Brooks
D) Mike Bellotti

49) Oregon had a winning percentage over .600 during the 1990s?

A) True
B) False

50) How many yards is the longest rushing play in Oregon history?

A) 76
B) 84
C) 92
D) 99

Second Quarter Duck Cool Fact

Before the current Duck mascot, Oregon sporting events were attended by a live-Duck mascot. This tradition began in the 1920s when a campus fraternity began bringing a duck named Puddles to Oregon football and basketball games. Puddles and his offspring represented Oregon sports until the 1940s. After several complaints from the Humane Society, the tradition of a live Duck was scrapped for the current costumed mascot used today.

Second Quarter Answer Key

1) C – 496 (Oregon scored 496 points in 13 games during the 2007 season, a 38.2 points per game average.)
2) A – 14 (Whittle wore the #14 at Oregon.)
3) D – 6 (QB Hugo Bezdek [1954], QB Norm Van Brocklin [1966], HB John Kitzmiller [1969], HB-T J.W. Beckett [1972], HB Mel Renfro [1986], and RB-WR Bobby Moore [2007])
4) C – 38 (Oregon is 38-0 all-time when scoring 50 points in a game.)
5) A – True (Whitehead had 192 carries for 737 yards in 2003, 200 carries for 1,144 yards in 2004, and 156 carries for 679 yards in 2005 to lead Oregon.)
6) B – 3 (1895 [4-0], 1906 [5-0-1], and 1916 [7-0-1])
7) B – 1899 (Oregon played California at Berkeley in 1899. Oregon 0, Cal 12)
8) C – Navy (Oregon is 8-3-1 all-time versus Air Force and 0-0-2 all-time versus Army.)
9) B – No (Oregon's highest rushing total is 465 yards at Washington in 2007. Oregon 55, Washington 34)
10) A – San Jose State (In 18 meetings, Oregon is 12-6 versus the Spartans.)
11) B – .541 (Oregon is 55-46-10 all-time versus Oregon State.)

12) D – Danny O'Neil (O'Neil completed 41 of 61 passes for 465 yards versus Penn State in the 1995 Rose Bowl. Oregon 20, Penn State 38)

13) A – 3 (Oregon owns a 2-1 record when ESPN's *College Gameday* visits Eugene.)

14) C – 2000 (Oregon went 10-2 in 2000, including a 35-30 victory over Texas in the Holiday Bowl.)

15) D – 56 (Oregon 56, Oregon State 14 at Oregon in 2005)

16) B – George Shaw (Shaw had 18 interceptions at Oregon from 1951-1954.)

17) C – 95 yards (Tom Blanchard threw a 95-yard touchdown pass to Bob Newland at Illinois in 1970. Oregon 16, Illinois 20)

18) A – Joe Sheffeld Award (DT Leie Sualua won the first award in 1998. The Ed Moshofsky Award is given to Oregon's top offensive lineman.)

19) D – 12 (Oregon has had 12 players drafted in the first round of the NFL Draft, including Jonathan Stewart in 2008.)

20) B – False (Oregon is 8-13 all-time in bowl games.)

21) C – Dan Fouts (Fouts was 188-361 for 2,390 yards and 16 touchdowns in 1970.)

22) D – Rose Bowl (Oregon's first bowl appearance was in the 1917 Rose Bowl, a 14-0 victory over Pennsylvania.)

23) B – 1965 (Steve Bunker had 5 receptions for 127 yards and Ray Palm had 7 receptions for 104 yards versus Oregon State in 1965. Oregon 14, Oregon State 19)

24) A – Gregg McCallum (McCallum made 24 field goals in 32 attempts in 1989.)

25) A – 1955 (Oregon averaged 252.7 yards per game on the ground in 1955.)

26) A – 1919 (Oregon finished the 1919 season 5-1-3 and shared the Pacific Coast Conference crown.)

27) B – 3 (Oregon finished the 1948 season ranked #9, the 2000 season ranked #7, and the 2001 season ranked #2.)

28) C – Track and Field (Renfro was named All-American in 1962 after finishing 2nd in the NCAA in the 120-yard high hurdles.)

29) C – UC Davis

30) A – 4 (Oregon went 1-2-1 in their first season in 1894.)

31) D – Pat Johnson (Johnson had 199 yards receiving versus the Beavers in 1997. Oregon 48, Oregon State 30)

32) C – Big East (Oregon is 5-2 [.714] all-time versus the Big East Conference.)

33) A – Jack Morris (Morris rushed for 212 yards at USC in 1957. Oregon 16, USC 7)

34) B – Bob Berry (Berry threw for 1,675 yards in 1963 and 1,478 yards in 1964.)

35) D – Oregon State (Oregon 0, Oregon State 16 in 1894)

36) B – 1972 (Bobby Moore was selected #4 overall by the St. Louis Cardinals and Tom Drougas was selected #22 overall by the Baltimore Colts.)

37) A – 1964 (Oregon's defense gave up 94 points in 10 games, a 9.4 average per game.)

38) C – 11 (Burwell rushed for 100 yards 11 times during his Duck career from 1990-1993.)

39) B – Akili Smith (Smith was 215-371 for 3,763 yards in 1998.)

40) A – True (Moore caught 54 passes for 786 yards and scored 96 points to lead the conference in 1969.)

41) C – Tony Hartley (Hartley had 242 receiving yards versus Washington in 1998. Oregon 27, Washington 22)

42) D – 7 (Bob Newland 1,123 yards in 1970, Sammie Parker 1,88 yards in 2003, Pat Johnson 1,072 yards in 1997, Demetrius Williams 1,059 yards in 2005, Damon Griffin 1,038 yards in 1998, Cristin McLemore 1,036 yards in 1995, and Tony Hartley 1,015 yards in 1999)

43) A – Jake Leicht (Leicht was named All-American in 1945 after recording 10 interceptions.)

44) B – 2 (1994 and 2001)

45) A – 0 (Oregon currently has 0 retired numbers.)

46) B – 44 (Oregon scored 44 points in their first season, all in their first game.)

47) C – Paul Martinez (Martinez was 6-6 versus Montana in 2005. Oregon 47, Montana 14)

48) D – Mike Bellotti (Bellotti won his Oregon coaching debut in 1995. Oregon 27, Utah 20)

49) B – False (The Ducks were 70-48 during the 1990s, a .593 winning percentage.)

50) C – 92 (Bob Smith had a 92-yard touchdown run versus Idaho in 1938. Oregon 19, Idaho 6)

Note: All answers valid as of the end of the 2007 season, unless otherwise indicated in the question itself.

Third Quarter

3-Point Questions

1) Oregon's Gordon E. Wilson Award is presented annually to which player?

A) Top Special Teams Performer
B) Top Defensive Back
C) Top Scholar-Athlete
D) Top Freshman Performer

2) What is the Oregon record for most tackles in a single season?

A) 140
B) 162
C) 184
D) 206

3) Where did Oregon play its home games before Autzen Stadium opened?

A) Alumni Stadium
B) Oregon Park
C) Hayward Field
D) Duck Stadium

4) Which Duck head coach has the second highest total wins in team history?

A) Hugo Bezdek
B) Rich Brooks
C) Len Casanova
D) John McEwan

5) What was the largest margin of victory for Oregon in a bowl game?

A) 24
B) 30
C) 35
D) 41

6) Who holds the Oregon record for receiving yards in a career?

A) Bob Newland
B) Sammie Parker
C) Bobby Moore
D) Anthony Jones

7) Which of the following Oregon QBs NEVER threw 20 touchdown passes in a single season?

A) Danny O'Neil
B) Jason Fife
C) Kellen Clemens
D) Chris Miller

8) How many combined kickoffs and punts were returned for touchdowns by the Ducks in 2007?

A) 0
B) 1
C) 2
D) 3

9) Who is the only Oregon player to intercept 4 passes in a single game?

A) Shy Huntington
B) Chad Cota
C) Bill Drake
D) Herman O'Berry

10) Who was the first Oregon player to be featured on the cover of *Sports Illustrated*?

A) George Shaw
B) Bobby Moore
C) Joey Harrington
D) Akili Smith

11) How many times has Oregon beaten Washington and Washington State in the same season?

A) 14 times
B) 28 times
C) 42 times
D) 56 times

12) How many games did Akili Smith pass for more than 300 yards in 1998?

A) 3
B) 5
C) 7
D) 10

13) How many Oregon players have been named first team Academic All-American?

A) 4
B) 6
C) 9
D) 11

14) What is the Oregon record for career touchdown receptions?

A) 17
B) 21
C) 24
D) 29

15) Which Oregon coach has the best winning percentage (minimum 3 seasons)?

A) Rich Brooks
B) Len Casanova
C) Jim Aiken
D) Mike Bellotti

16) What are the most rushing yards given up by Oregon in a game at Autzen Stadium?

A) 450 yards
B) 482 yards
C) 524 yards
D) 541 yards

17) Who was the last Oregon player to record over 100 solo tackles in a single season?

A) Mark Kearns
B) David Moretti
C) Chris Cosgrove
D) Jeff Sherman

18) What are the most points scored by Oregon in a game at Autzen Stadium?

A) 61
B) 68
C) 72
D) 77

19) When was the last time the season-leading passer for Oregon had less than 1,000 yards passing?

A) 1953
B) 1969
C) 1978
D) 1991

20) How many times did a Rich Brooks coached Oregon team shutout their opponents?

A) 0
B) 6
C) 13
D) 19

21) Who was the last Oregon player to lead the team in rushing and receiving in the same season?

A) Bobby Moore
B) Sean Burwell
C) Maurice Morris
D) Dino Philyaw

22) When was the last time an Oregon game ended in a tie?

A) 1952
B) 1966
C) 1971
D) 1983

23) Has Oregon ever lost 10 games in a season?

A) Yes
B) No

24) Who was the first consensus All-American running back at Oregon?

A) Bobby Moore
B) Mel Renfro
C) Mike Mikulak
D) Jake Leicht

25) Oregon's defense has never given up 500 yards passing in a game at Autzen Stadium.

A) True
B) False

26) Who was the first All-American linebacker at Oregon?

A) Joe Farwell
B) Bruce Beekley
C) Chris Cosgrove
D) Never had an All-American linebacker

27) What are the fewest rushing yards given up by Oregon in a single game?

A) -47
B) -21
C) 6
D) 19

28) Who was the last receiver to lead the Ducks in scoring?

A) Keenan Howry
B) Bob Newland
C) Darrell Robinson
D) Pat Johnson

29) How many Oregon players have been named All-American more than once?

A) 0
B) 2
C) 4
D) 6

30) What was the combined winning percentage of coaches who lasted just one season at Oregon?

A) .404
B) .494
C) .537
D) .579

31) Against which team did Oregon get their first Pac-10 win?

A) California
B) Oregon State
C) USC
D) Washington

32) What is Oregon's longest drought between bowl games?

A) 13 years
B) 20 years
C) 28 years
D) 33 years

33) How long is the longest field goal ever kicked by an Oregon player?

A) 52 yards
B) 55 yards
C) 59 yards
D) 62 yards

34) Dan Fouts was drafted in which round of the 1973 NFL Draft?

A) 1
B) 3
C) 5
D) 7

35) Has an Oregon player ever scored more than six touchdowns in a game?

A) Yes
B) No

36) What is the Oregon record for receptions by a Duck in a Rose Bowl game?

A) 7
B) 9
C) 11
D) 13

Third Quarter

3-Point Questions

37) In 1895, which team did Oregon beat twice?

A) Portland
B) Williamette
C) California
D) Albany College

38) Who is the last Duck to lead the team in receiving for three straight seasons?

A) Terry Obee
B) Greg Moser
C) Sammie Parker
D) Cristin McLemore

39) In which season did the Ducks average the most points per game?

A) 1991
B) 1998
C) 2001
D) 2007

40) When was the last time the leading rusher for Oregon gained less than 500 yards for the season?

A) 1963
B) 1980
C) 1993
D) 2004

41) Which Oregon quarterback threw the most career touchdown passes?

A) Bill Musgrave
B) A.J. Feeley
C) Danny O'Neil
D) Kellen Clemens

42) Who holds the Oregon record for the longest fumble recovery returned for a touchdown?

A) Kenny Wheaton
B) Mario Clark
C) J.W. Beckett
D) Jim Smith

43) What position did Coach Rich Brooks play in college?

A) Quarterback
B) Defensive Back
C) Fullback
D) Linebacker

44) Who coached Oregon in their first Pac-10 season?

A) Len Casanova
B) Jerry Frei
C) John Warren
D) Don Read

45) In which bowl game, other than the Rose Bowl, did Oregon first appear?

A) Sun Bowl
B) Cotton Bowl
C) Orange Bowl
D) Liberty Bowl

46) Oregon has a better than .500 winning percentage at Autzen Stadium.

A) True
B) False

47) Who is the only Duck receiver to catch four touchdown passes in a game?

A) Demetrius Williams
B) Bob Newland
C) Cristin McLemore
D) Keenan Howry

48) Who was the first African American to be named All-American at Oregon?

A) Jim Smith
B) Bobby Moore
C) Mel Renfro
D) Alex Molden

49) Joey Harrington threw more than 60 touchdown passes in his Oregon career.

A) True
B) False

50) What is the Oregon record for consecutive bowl losses?

A) 1
B) 3
C) 4
D) 6

Third Quarter Duck Cool Fact

In November of 2007, a then record crowd of 59,277, wild fans packed Autzen Stadium to watch #5 Oregon battle #12 USC. Oregon took the lead early and never looked back in a 24-17 victory. During that game, the crowd noise was recorded at 127.2 decibels making Autzen Stadium the loudest stadium in college football, topping the 126 decibels recorded at Clemson's Memorial Stadium.

Third Quarter Answer Key

1) A – Top Special Teams Performer (The award is named after Gordon Wilson, an Oregon football letterman in 1923 and 1924. Tommy Thompson won the first award in 1992.)
2) D – 206 (Tom Graham recorded 206 tackles for Oregon in 1969.)
3) C – Hayward Field (Oregon played its home games at Hayward Field [capacity 15,000] from 1919-1966.)
4) B – Rich Brooks (Brooks won 91 games at Oregon from 1977-1994.)
5) C – 35 points (Oregon 56, South Florida 21 in the 2007 Sun Bowl)
6) B – Sammie Parker (Parker racked up 2,761 receiving yards at Oregon from 2000-2003.)
7) D – Chris Miller (Miller's highest total came in 1985 when he threw 18 touchdown passes.)
8) A – 0
9) A – Shy Huntington (Huntington intercepted 4 passes versus Penn in the 1917 Rose Bowl.)
10) D – Akili Smith (Smith was featured on the cover of *Sports Illustrated* in April of 1999.)
11) A – 14 times (Oregon has beaten Washington and Washington State in the same season 14 times, including 2007.)

12) B – 5 (Smith threw for 300 yards 5 times during the 1998 season.)

13) B – 6 (Steve Barnett [1962], Tim Casey [1965], Mike Preacher [1986], Bill Musgrave [1990], Ryan Schmid [2000, 2001], and Joey Harrington [2001])

14) C – 24 (This record is shared by two Oregon receivers. Cristin McLemore caught 24 touchdown passes from 1992-1995, and Keenan Howry equaled the mark from 1999-2002.)

15) D – Mike Bellotti (Bellotti has a .671 winning percentage since taking over at Oregon in 1995.)

16) C – 524 yards (Washington State rolled up 524 rushing yards versus the Ducks in 1984. Oregon 41, WSU 50)

17) A – Mark Kearns (Kearns recorded 100 solo tackles [131 total] in 1989.)

18) C – 72 (Oregon 72, Nevada 10 in 1999)

19) D – 1991 (Danny O'Neil completed 55 of 115 passes for 713 yards to lead the Ducks in 1991.)

20) B – 6 (Between 1977 and 1994, Oregon recorded 6 shutouts under Brooks, outscoring those opponents a combined 165-0.)

21) B – Sean Burwell (Burwell had 193 carries for 822 yards and caught 35 passes for 293 yards to lead the Ducks in 1992.)

22) D – 1983 (Oregon 0, Oregon State 0)

23) B – No (Oregon has lost 9 games in a season a few times, but never 10.)

24) C – Mike Mikulak (1933)

25) B – False (Arizona State holds the Autzen Stadium record, passing for 559 yards versus Oregon in 2002. Oregon 42, ASU 45)

26) D – Never had an All-American linebacker

27) A – -47 (Oregon held BYU to -47 rushing yards in 1990. Oregon 32, BYU 16)

28) A – Keenan Howry (Howry scored 72 points [12 touchdowns] in 2001 to tie for the team lead with kicker Jared Siegel.)

29) B – 2 (Tackle Steve Barnett in 1961 & 1962 and halfback Mel Renfro in 1962 and 1963.)

30) C – .537 (Oregon's one-year coaches were a combined 45-38-12, a .537 winning percentage.)

31) D – Washington (Oregon 7, Washington 0 in 1964)

32) C – 28 years (Oregon did not appear in a bowl game following the 1920-1947 seasons.)

33) C – 59 yards (Jared Siegel booted a 59-yard field goal at UCLA in 2002. Oregon 31, UCLA 30)

34) B – 3 (Fouts was drafted by San Diego in the 3rd round of the 1973 NFL Draft. Fouts went on to pass for more than 43,000 yards on his way to the NFL Hall of Fame.)

35) A – Yes (Charles Taylor scored 10 touchdowns in a game versus Puget Sound in 1910.)

36) C – 11 (Josh Wilcox caught 11 passes for 135 yards in the 1995 Rose Bowl.)

37) B – Williamette (Oregon beat Williamette 8-4 and 6-0 in 1895.)

38) A – Terry Obee (Obee caught 33 passes for 640 yards in 1987, 33 passes for 596 yards in 1988, and 46 passes for 741 yards in 1989.)

39) B – 1998 (The Ducks scored 473 points in 12 games, a 39.4 average per game.)

40) C – 1993 (Sean Burwell had 113 carries for 457 yards to lead the Ducks in 1993.)

41) C – Danny O'Neil (O'Neil threw 62 touchdown passes for Oregon from 1991-1994.)

42) D – Jim Smith (Jim "Yazoo" Smith 99 yards versus Oregon State in 1966. Oregon 15, Oregon State 20)

43) B – Defensive Back (Brooks played defensive back at Oregon State from 1961-1963.)

44) A – Len Casanova (Casanova led the Ducks to a 7-2-1 record in 1964.)

45) B – Cotton Bowl (Oregon appeared in the 1949 Cotton Bowl, a 13-21 loss to Southern Methodist.)

46) A – True (Oregon is 140-90-5 all-time at Autzen Stadium, a .606 winning percentage.)

47) D – Keenan Howry (Howry caught 4 touchdown passes versus Arizona State in 2001.)

48) C – Mel Renfro (1962)

49) B – False (Harrington threw 59 touchdown passes for Oregon from 1998-2001.)

50) C – 4 (Oregon has lost 4 consecutive bowl games on 3 separate occasions, most recently the 2002 Seattle Bowl, the 2005 Holiday Bowl, and the 2006 Las Vegas Bowl.)

Note: All answers valid as of the end of the 2007 season, unless otherwise indicated in the question itself.

1) Who is Oregon's all-time sacks leader?

A) Saul Patu
B) Anthony Trucks
C) Reggie Jordan
D) Ernest Jones

2) Of the following Oregon opponents, which is the only one the Ducks HAVE beaten?

A) Ohio State
B) Nebraska
C) Wake Forest
D) Kansas

3) What is the worst defeat Oregon has suffered in a bowl game?

A) 26 points
B) 29 points
C) 32 points
D) 37 points

4) No Oregon player has recorded 400 tackles in his career.

A) True
B) False

5) Which coach had the worst winning percentage at Oregon (minimum 3 seasons)?

A) Jerry Frei
B) Prink Callison
C) Tex Oliver
D) Don Read

6) Who holds the Oregon record for receptions in a season?

A) Jaison Williams
B) Steve Bunker
C) Sammie Parker
D) Cristin McLemore

7) What is the Oregon record for consecutive seasons appearing in a bowl game?

A) 7
B) 9
C) 12
D) 15

8) How many Oregon coaches are in the College Football Hall of Fame?

A) 0
B) 1
C) 2
D) 3

9) How many former Ducks are in the Pro Football Hall of Fame?

A) 2
B) 4
C) 6
D) 8

10) Which Duck blocked Oklahoma's last-second field goal attempt in the controversial 2006 game?

A) J.D. Nelson
B) Blair Phillips
C) Dexter Manley
D) Patrick Chung

11) Which Oregon player holds the record for career yards per carry average?

A) John McKay
B) Onterrio Smith
C) Mel Renfro
D) Jonathan Stewart

12) How many times has Oregon shutout their opponents?

A) 120
B) 141
C) 164
D) 187

13) What is the Oregon record for pass completions in a single game?

A) 29
B) 37
C) 41
D) 50

14) Who holds the Oregon single season rushing record?

A) Onterrio Smith
B) Jonathan Stewart
C) Saladin McCollough
D) Bobby Moore

15) When was the last time the Ducks were shutout?

A) 1982
B) 1993
C) 2001
D) 2007

16) Has Oregon ever played a game outside of the United States?

A) Yes
B) No

17) In which season did the first African-American(s) play for Oregon?

A) 1904
B) 1917
C) 1926
D) 1941

18) Who did Oregon play in their longest game in history?

A) Clemson
B) USC
C) Washington
D) Arizona

19) Who holds the record for career rushing touchdowns at Oregon?

A) Saladin McCollough
B) Terrence Whitehead
C) Ricky Whittle
D) Derek Loville

20) Who was the last Oregon quarterback to lead the team in scoring?

A) Reggie Ogburn
B) Joey Harrington
C) Jack Henderson
D) George Shaw

Fourth Quarter *4-Point Questions*

21) How many all-time head coaches has Oregon had?

A) 17
B) 22
C) 26
D) 31

22) What is the largest margin of victory for Oregon against Oregon State?

A) 23
B) 35
C) 44
D) 51

23) Which coach has the second best winning percentage at Oregon (minimum 3 seasons)?

A) Len Casanova
B) Hugo Bezdek
C) John McEwan
D) Shy Huntington

24) Has Oregon played every Big Ten team at least once?

A) Yes
B) No

25) Who was the first Oregon coach to win the Paul "Bear" Bryant Award?

A) Mike Bellotti
B) Len Casanova
C) Rich Brooks
D) Has Never Happened

26) Against which BCS Conference does Oregon have the worst winning percentage?

A) Big Ten
B) Big 12
C) Big East
D) SEC

27) What are the most interceptions thrown by Oregon in a single game?

A) 6
B) 7
C) 8
D) 9

28) How many times has Oregon won nine or more games in a season?

A) 8
B) 10
C) 12
D) 15

29) What decade did Oregon have its worst winning percentage?

A) 1930s
B) 1950s
C) 1970s
D) 1980s

30) Has Oregon ever given up 50 or more points in a game that they won?

A) Yes
B) No

31) Who holds the Oregon record for tackles for loss in a season?

A) Marcus Woods
B) Kevin Mitchell
C) Jeff Cummins
D) Reggie Jordan

32) What are the most consecutive wins for Oregon versus Oregon State?

A) 3
B) 5
C) 8
D) 10

33) Who was the last Oregon player to lead the team in tackles and interceptions in the same season?

A) Joe Farwell
B) Chris Oldham
C) Aaron Gipson
D) Kenny Wheaton

34) Have Oregon and Oregon State ever played at a neutral site?

A) Yes
B) No

35) Which team has Oregon played the most on homecoming?

A) Washington State
B) UCLA
C) Arizona
D) Oregon State

36) How many times has Oregon appeared in the Rose Bowl?

A) 2
B) 4
C) 6
D) 8

Fourth Quarter

4-Point Questions

37) How many Oregon players have won the Morris Trophy?

A) 2
B) 4
C) 6
D) 8

38) Who was the first All-American lineman at Oregon?

A) Gary Zimmerman
B) Dave Wilcox
C) Steve Barnett
D) Tom Drougas

39) Who holds the Oregon career record for average yards per punt?

A) Henry Parks
B) Josh Bidwell
C) Kevin Hicks
D) Len Isberg

40) Every 300+ yard passing game by a Duck quarterback has taken place since 1980.

A) True
B) False

41) Which Oregon quarterback never threw for 450 yards in a single game?

A) Joey Harrington
B) Ryan Perry-Smith
C) Bill Musgrave
D) Akili Smith

42) How many times has an Oregon player scored 100 or more points in a season?

A) 1
B) 2
C) 3
D) 4

43) When was the last time Oregon returned a punt for a touchdown?

A) 1997
B) 1999
C) 2003
D) 2006

44) What was the best winning percentage of an Oregon head coach who lasted only one season?

A) .650
B) .800
C) .925
D) 1.000

Fourth Quarter *4-Point Questions*

45) When was the last time the Ducks shutout an opponent?

A) 1985
B) 1996
C) 2003
D) 2006

46) Who holds the Oregon record for rushing touchdowns in a season?

A) Derek Loville
B) Jonathan Stewart
C) Ricky Whittle
D) Saladin McCollough

47) Which Oregon quarterback threw the most career interceptions?

A) Dan Fouts
B) Danny O'Neil
C) George Shaw
D) Bill Musgrave

48) What is the Oregon record for most consecutive wins?

A) 8
B) 11
C) 15
D) 19

49) In which season did Oregon give up the most points?

A) 1959
B) 1977
C) 1988
D) 2003

50) Who is the only player in Oregon history to return a kickoff 100 yards for a touchdown?

A) Chris Oldham
B) Steve Brown
C) Kenny Washington
D) Woodley Lewis

Fourth Quarter Duck Cool Fact

The University of Oregon campus has been used in the filming of several movies including *Abe Lincoln in Illinois* (1940), *Five Easy Pieces* (1971), *Stand By Me* (1986) and *Without Limits* (1998). However, the most famous is the 1978 classic *Animal House.* Although 12 colleges in six different states said no, Oregon President William Boyd agreed to let John Landis film on campus without even reading the script. Several campus buildings appeared in the film including the Phi Kappa Psi house, Johnson Hall, the Fishbowl Dining Area and the Sigma Nu frat house which hosted the infamous Toga Party. In one scene Pinto was making out with the Mayor's daughter Clorette. That scene took place on the 50-yard line of Autzen Stadium.

Fourth Quarter Answer Key

1) D – Ernest Jones (Jones recorded 29 quarterback sacks at Oregon from 1990-1993.)
2) B – Nebraska (Oregon is 1-5 all-time versus Nebraska. The Ducks are a combined 0-10-1 versus the other three opponents.)
3) C – 32 points (Oregon 6, Colorado 38 in the 1996 Cotton Bowl)
4) B – False (Oregon has 2 players with more than 400 career tackles. Tom Graham had 433 tackles from 1969-1971 and Bruce Beekley had 429 tackles from 1976-1978.)
5) D – Don Read (Read was 9-24 [.273] at Oregon from 1974-1976.)
6) C – Sammie Parker (Parker caught 77 passes for the Ducks in 2003.)
7) A – 7 (Oregon made a bowl appearance in 7 consecutive seasons from 1997-2003.)
8) B – 1 (Len Casanova was inducted into the College Football Hall of Fame in 1977.)
9) C – 6 (Norm Van Brocklin [1971], Tuffy Leemans [1978], Dan Fouts [1993], Mel Renfro [1996], Dave Wilcox [2000], and Gary Zimmerman [2008])

10) B – Blair Phillips (Phillips blocked the Sooners' 44-yard field goal attempt on the last play of the game to preserve a 34-33 Ducks win.)

11) A – John McKay (McKay, better known for his coaching career, averaged 6.1 yards per carry at Oregon from 1948-1949.)

12) D – 187 (Oregon has registered 187 shutouts in its history.)

13) C – 41 (Danny O'Neil completed 41 of 61 passes versus Penn State in the 1995 Rose Bowl.)

14) B – Jonathan Stewart (Stewart rushed for 1,722 yards for the Ducks in 2007.)

15) D – 2007 (Oregon 0, UCLA 16)

16) A – Yes (Oregon played USC in Tokyo, Japan in November of 1985. Oregon 6, USC 20)

17) C – 1926 (Robert Robinson and Charles Williams were the first African-Americans to play football at Oregon, joining the team in 1926.)

18) B – USC (Oregon beat USC 33-30 in 3 overtimes in 1999.)

19) D – Derek Loville (Loville racked up 41 career rushing touchdowns at Oregon from 1986-1989.)

20) A – Reggie Ogburn (Ogburn scored 42 points to lead the Ducks in 1980.)

21) D – 31 (Mike Bellotti became Oregon's 31st head coach in February of 1995.)

22) C – 44 (This has happened twice; Oregon beat Oregon State 46-2 in 1895 and 44-0 in 1987.)

23) B – Hugo Bezdek (Bezdek had a .697 winning percentage [25-10-3] at Oregon from 1913-1917.)

24) A – Yes (Oregon has played every Big Ten team and is 13-26 all-time versus the Big Ten.)

25) C – Rich Brooks (Brooks won the award as National Coach of the Year in 1994 after leading the Ducks to a 9-4 record.)

26) B – Big 12 (Oregon is 12-25-1 all-time versus the Big 12, a .329 winning percentage.)

27) D – 9 (Oregon threw 9 interceptions versus Washington in 1952. Oregon 0, Washington 49)

28) B – 10 (1928, 1933, 1948, 1994, 1995, 1999, 2000, 2001, 2005, and 2007)

29) C – 1970s (Oregon was 36-75-1 during the 1970s, a .326 winning percentage.)

30) A – Yes (Oregon beat Arizona State 56-55 in 2000.)

31) B – Kevin Mitchell (Mitchell had 23 tackles for loss for the Ducks in 2001.)

32) C – 8 (Oregon beat Oregon State 8 consecutive times from 1975-1982.)

33) D – Kenny Wheaton (Wheaton led the Ducks with 73 tackles and 2 interceptions in 1996.)

34) A – Yes (The Civil War game has been played at Albany twice [1912 and1913] and at Portland 7 times [1908, 1917, 1933, 1934, 1938, 1950, and 1952].)

35) A – Washington State (Oregon has played Washington State 16 times on homecoming, compiling a 7-7-2 record.)

36) B – 4 (Oregon has a 1-3 record in 4 Rose Bowl appearances [1917, 1920, 1958, and 1995].)

37) B – 4 (Vince Goldsmith [1980], Gary Zimmerman [1983], Adam Snyder [2004], and Haloti Ngata [2005])

38) C – Steve Barnett (Tackle Steve Barnett was named All-American in 1961.)

39) D – Len Isberg (Isberg averaged 42.8 yards per punt at Oregon.)

40) B – False (Dan Fouts was 28-43 for 396 yards and 4 touchdowns versus Air Force in 1970.)

41) A – Joey Harrington (Harrington's career high was 434 yards at Arizona State in 2000.)

42) C – 3 (Nathan Villegas scored 117 points in 1998, Jared Siegel scored 109 points in 2002, and Greg McCallum scored 109 points in 1989.)

43) D – 2006 (Patrick Chung returned a punt 59 yards for a touchdown versus Washington in 2006. Oregon 34, Washington 14)

44) D – 1.000 (Oregon was 4-0 in 1895 under Percy Benson.)
45) C – 2003 (Oregon 35, Stanford 0)
46) D – Saladin McCollough (McCollough rushed for 15 touchdowns in 1996.)
47) A – Dan Fouts (Fouts threw 54 interceptions at Oregon from 1970-1972.)
48) B – 11 (Oregon won the last 5 games of the 2001 season and the first 6 games of the 2002 season.)
49) B – 1977 (Oregon gave up 377 points in 11 games [33.4 average per game] during a 2-9 1977 season.)
50) D – Woodley Lewis (Lewis returned a kickoff 102 yards for a touchdown versus Colorado in 1949.)

Note: All answers valid as of the end of the 2007 season, unless otherwise indicated in the question itself.

Overtime Bonus *4-Point Questions*

1) Which coach has the second longest tenure at Oregon?

A) Prink Callison
B) Jim Aiken
C) Mike Bellotti
D) Len Casanova

2) What is the longest winning streak for the Ducks in the Oregon-Washington series?

A) 2
B) 4
C) 7
D) 9

3) Which Oregon quarterback WAS NOT picked in the first round of the NFL Draft?

A) George Shaw
B) Akili Smith
C) Norm Van Brocklin
D) Chris Miller

4) Shy Huntington is the first person to play for and coach the same school in the Rose Bowl.

A) True
B) False

Overtime Bonus *4-Point Questions*

5) What is Oregon's all-time winning percentage in overtime games?

A) .385
B) .475
C) .600
D) .750

6) Who was the first Oregon player to declare early for the NFL Draft?

A) Akili Smith
B) Kenny Wheaton
C) Mel Renfro
D) Gary Zimmerman

7) What is the largest crowd ever to see an Oregon game?

A) 98,244
B) 100,601
C) 104,206
D) 109,733

8) Has Oregon ever beaten Oregon State twice in the same season?

A) Yes
B) No

9) What are the most consecutive times Oregon has been shutout?

A) 2
B) 3
C) 5
D) 8

10) What are the most points scored by Oregon in a single game?

A) 76
B) 88
C) 100
D) 115

Overtime Bonus Answer Key

1) D – Len Casanova (Casanova spent 16 seasons at Oregon from 1951-1966.)
2) B – 4 (Oregon is currently in the midst of their longest winning streak versus the Huskies. Oregon has won the last 4 meetings form 2004-2007.)
3) C – Norm Van Brocklin (NFL Hall of Famer Norm Van Brocklin was drafted in the 4th round of the 1949 NFL Draft by Los Angeles.)
4) A – True (Huntington played for Oregon in the 1917 Rose Bowl and coached them in it in 1920.)
5) C – .600 (Oregon is 6-4 all-time since the inception of overtime in college football.)
6) B – Kenny Wheaton (He declared early for the 1997 NFL Draft and was selected in the 3rd round by Dallas.)
7) D – 109,733 (They packed "The Big House" in Ann Arbor to watch Oregon whip Michigan 39-7 in 2007.)
8) A – Yes (Oregon beat Oregon State 2-0 & 12-8 in 1896.)
9) C – 5 (Oregon was shutout in the last 5 games of 1936.)
10) D – 115 (Oregon beat Puget Sound 115-0 in 1910.)

Note: All answers valid as of the end of the 2007 season, unless otherwise indicated in the question itself.

Player / Team Score Sheet

DUCKOLOGY TRIVIA CHALLENGE

Name:__________________________________

First Quarter				Second Quarter				Third Quarter				Fourth Quarter				Overtime	
1		26		1		26		1		26		1		26		1	
2		27		2		27		2		27		2		27		2	
3		28		3		28		3		28		3		28		3	
4		29		4		29		4		29		4		29		4	
5		30		5		30		5		30		5		30		5	
6		31		6		31		6		31		6		31		6	
7		32		7		32		7		32		7		32		7	
8		33		8		33		8		33		8		33		8	
9		34		9		34		9		34		9		34		9	
10		35		10		35		10		35		10		35		10	
11		36		11		36		11		36		11		36			
12		37		12		37		12		37		12		37			
13		38		13		38		13		38		13		38			
14		39		14		39		14		39		14		39			
15		40		15		40		15		40		15		40			
16		41		16		41		16		41		16		41			
17		42		17		42		17		42		17		42			
18		43		18		43		18		43		18		43			
19		44		19		44		19		44		19		44			
20		45		20		45		20		45		20		45			
21		46		21		46		21		46		21		46			
22		47		22		47		22		47		22		47			
23		48		23		48		23		48		23		48			
24		49		24		49		24		49		24		49			
25		50		25		50		25		50		25		50			
__x 1 =__				__x 2 =__				__x 3 =__				__x 4 =__				__x 4 =__	

Multiply total number correct by point value/quarter to calculate totals for each quarter.

Add total of all quarters below.

Total Points:_______

Thank you for playing Duckology Trivia Challenge.

Additional score sheets are available at:
www.TriviaGameBooks.com

Player / Team Score Sheet

DUCKOLOGY TRIVIA CHALLENGE

Name:____________________________________

First Quarter				Second Quarter				Third Quarter				Fourth Quarter				Overtime	
1		26		1		26		1		26		1		26		1	
2		27		2		27		2		27		2		27		2	
3		28		3		28		3		28		3		28		3	
4		29		4		29		4		29		4		29		4	
5		30		5		30		5		30		5		30		5	
6		31		6		31		6		31		6		31		6	
7		32		7		32		7		32		7		32		7	
8		33		8		33		8		33		8		33		8	
9		34		9		34		9		34		9		34		9	
10		35		10		35		10		35		10		35		10	
11		36		11		36		11		36		11		36			
12		37		12		37		12		37		12		37			
13		38		13		38		13		38		13		38			
14		39		14		39		14		39		14		39			
15		40		15		40		15		40		15		40			
16		41		16		41		16		41		16		41			
17		42		17		42		17		42		17		42			
18		43		18		43		18		43		18		43			
19		44		19		44		19		44		19		44			
20		45		20		45		20		45		20		45			
21		46		21		46		21		46		21		46			
22		47		22		47		22		47		22		47			
23		48		23		48		23		48		23		48			
24		49		24		49		24		49		24		49			
25		50		25		50		25		50		25		50			
__x 1 =__				__x 2 =__				__x 3 =__				__x 4 =__				__x 4 =__	

Multiply total number correct by point value/quarter to calculate totals for each quarter.

Add total of all quarters below.

Total Points:_______

Thank you for playing Duckology Trivia Challenge.

Additional score sheets are available at:
www.TriviaGameBooks.com